# DRAW LIKE AN EGYPTIAN

## Claire Thorne

THE BRITISH MUSEUM PRESS

© 2007 Claire Thorne

Published by British Museum Press
A division of The British Museum
Company Ltd
38 Russell Square, London
WC1B 3QQ

ISBN-13: 978-0-7141-3114-6

A catalogue record for this title is
available from the British Library.
Claire Thorne has asserted the
right to be identified as the author
of this work.

Designed by Herring Bone
Design Ltd
Printed and bound by Printing
Express in Hong Kong

All original illustrations are by
Claire Thorne. The line drawing
on pages 14–15 is after R.B.
Parkinson. The 'false door'
drawing on page 36 is based on
an illustration by T.G.H. James.

Photographs are © the Trustees of
the British Museum, unless
otherwise stated below:

Page 9 (bottom): reproduced by
courtesy of John Taylor.

Pages 10 (left), 46 (bottom left) by
Claire Thorne.

This book is dedicated to
Ella and Rona,
Sam, Nathalie and Harry

A big and warm thank you to Dr Richard Parkinson
for his invaluable and good-humoured guidance,
thanks also to my editor Carolyn Jones, and to
Tania Watkins for her help and for suggesting the
photo showing King Akhenaten.

Lastly, thanks to my partner Michael Woolcott for
his support, and for putting more than his fair share
of family meals on the table.

# Introduction

The Ancient Egyptians used a style of drawing and painting that lasted for over three thousand years. Paintings covered every surface, including the walls of tombs and temples. Painted scenes in tombs showed the tomb owner enjoying his life, which he hoped would continue forever, and worshipping the gods, with plenty of food and possessions, and servants to work for him.

The Egyptians drew things as they should be, not how they actually looked. So all women were beautiful and all men were handsome. Temples show pharaohs as great rulers, honouring the gods and displaying their wealth and power, but painting and design were also important in the lives of ordinary people. They decorated their homes, their furniture, pottery, boxes and jewellery. They also painted on papyri and drew sketches on flakes of stone and bits of pot.

In this book you can find out about the rules of Egyptian painting and learn how to draw and paint animals, people, plants, houses and much more. You will see how to begin with simple shapes and build up colour and detail. It's easy to get started.
Go on – draw like an Egyptian!

An Egyptian painting showing Libyan, Nubian, Cretan and Babylonian prisoners.
Foreigners such as these have very colourful and patterned clothes. The ruling Egyptians usually wear fine white linen clothes, with rich gold and inlaid jewellery.

The Egyptians often used grids to lay out scenes on walls and other surfaces. They dipped string into red paint and pressed it on to the surface to make the grids. The grids helped to make sure that people and gods were all drawn to scale.

## People

The Egyptians drew people almost like a diagram. They showed each part of the body in the most recognizable and typical view. People's skin colour varies - men were painted redder than women, and children were painted paler.

This is an unfinished carving on a stela (tombstone). The figures on the left are sketched out and the figures on the right are being carved. Can you see the grid?

The most important person is shown largest. Women are smaller than men and stand behind their husbands.

Mouths are shown from the side.

Shoulders are drawn front on.

Waists are drawn sideways, but with the belly button showing.

Hands are drawn with thumb, fingers and nails showing.

Legs are sideways on.

Feet are sideways, with the arches and big toe nails showing.

Heads are drawn sideways.

Eyes and eyebrows are drawn front on.

Working people face toward the most important person in the scene and are drawn much smaller.

Captions in hieroglyphs give people's names.

These are called register lines. They divide up the picture so that everything can be shown in the right size and position, in relation to everything else.

This is the man's son. He faces the same way and holds his father's staff, showing that he shares his status.

# Outdoor scenes

Most Egyptian tomb scenes concentrated on the human figure. There were no realistic landscapes with reflections in water or shadows under trees. Outdoor scenes were there so that the tomb owner could benefit from the wildlife or from farming in the afterlife. So these scenes often included fishing and fowling, agricultural activity, offerings to the gods, and gardens.

Gardens were shown with various fig and sycamore trees all laden with fruit at varying stages of ripeness. Leafy trees provided shade where people could sit. Look at these two examples and notice how the trees are arranged around the ponds.

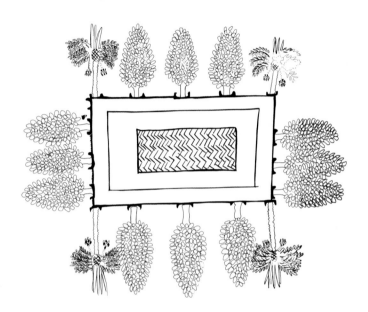

Garden ponds were shown from above, but with ducks and fishes shown sideways on.

This painting shows an official called Nakht fowling and fishing in the marshes. He is shown twice. He floats along on the boats, accompanied by his wife and children. The clump of papyrus reeds provides a background for both sides of the scene.

# Showing things clearly

It was important to show things clearly. The Egyptians drew the things inside boxes and containers as if they were outside and on top.

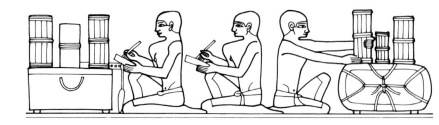

The top picture shows scribes at work. Bundles of rolled papyri are shown outside the cases, but in real life they would have been carried and stored inside them.

The picture below shows men carrying boxes which contain jewellery, a mirror, cosmetics and jars of ointment.

The Egyptians put top and side views together in the same drawing. This stool (below, left) is shown from the top and from the side. This is what it would have looked like in real life (below, right).

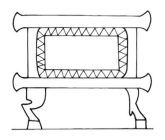 

The Ancient Egyptians did not want realistic views of things in the round and getting smaller at a distance (in perspective). To show things clearly, they set it all out in layers one above the other. A good example is Nebamun's offering table (above).

# More than one

The Ancient Egyptians had a formal way to show lots of animals, birds or people. This made it easy to draw many of the same thing.

One outline has been used several times to build up a picture of many cattle in a row. Only the colour and markings vary on each bull. They are all standing on the same register line.

Register line

Birds in a flock often have the same body shape. Only the wings differ, to give an impression of flight.

These men's individual features were not important, so the same outline has been repeated to show lots of men.

# Chaos

There are always exceptions to the rules! In battle and hunting scenes we see chaos instead of order and balance.

The scene below shows a sea battle against the Syrians. Unusually, bodies are flung about upside down and at all angles.

This shows a hunt in the desert. The broken and wavy register lines reflect the sandy hills and hollows of the desert, which the Egyptians saw as a dangerous and chaotic place.

# Lines and dots

The Ancient Egyptians built up their paintings by first drawing the shapes in red, then filling the shapes with colour, adding details in lines and dots, and finally drawing an outline in red or black. Pages 11, 12 and 13 will show you in more detail how to do the same thing.

Paint was made from stones and minerals found in Egypt. The stones were ground and mixed with plant gum or animal glue to form a smooth paste.

The Egyptians made brushes by shaping and splitting palm ribs and reeds. They used lines and dots to give a sense of texture. Here are some examples from paintings.

Feathers

Fish scales

Crocodile skin

Fur

Snake skin

They drew lines up and down, across and diagonally, which gives Egyptian paintings a lively look.

The Egyptians used geometric shapes and bold designs. You can see them here in a starlit sky, a dom-palm tree, desert plants, marshes and water.

# Exceptions and surprises

Egyptian art can look stiff to us, as if they drew using a rulebook, but there are always surprises. Look at the comical animals on the papyrus and the lively sketch on the flake of limestone. There are also exceptions to the rules – for example, a face shown in front view, or a king with a sagging belly!

Stick-men were a quick and expressive way of drawing spells and journeys.

Part of a papyrus painted with animals playing games and acting like humans.

A flake of limestone with an artist's practice drawing.

King Akhenaten broke from the traditional styles and had himself portrayed with a long face and drooping chin, narrow shoulders and a sagging belly.

A scene from the underworld with stick-men painted in red and black. It is painted on a tomb wall, but copies a style of painting found on papyri.

A rare example of a face shown from the front. This is a musician, painted on a tomb wall.

# Using modern paints and techniques

Here are some examples using modern paints and materials to create an Egyptian look. Try using pens or felt-tips over a wash of watercolour paint, or using wax crayons with watercolour washes over the top. Wait until the first wash has dried before applying the second. Experiment with inks, paints, pens and water-soluble crayons and use the best quality paper that you can afford. Smooth paper is easier for adding lots of detail.

Watercolour paper.
Paper is measured by weight in grams (gsm). Watercolour paint works better on thick heavy paper such as 300gsm or more, so that it doesn't go lumpy or bumpy.

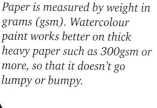

Ink

Felt pen

Art pen

mapping pen

Wax crayon

Water-soluble crayon

Crayon

Pans of watercolour

Sheets of papyrus are available at some art shops or specialist paper shops or museums.

Gouache

Acrylic gouache

Acrylic

Art pen on dry watercolour.

White and blue wax crayons, then two washes of brown watercolour.

Blue water-soluble crayon, yellow wax crayon and watercolour.

Mapping pen with blue ink over crayon on very smooth paper.

Build up the colour in crayons by shading in all directions.

Inks watered down. Overlapping blue, yellow and red makes green, orange and mauve.

Use felt-tip pens with brush and water.

Gouache.

Acrylic paint on papyrus.

You can blend water-soluble crayons with a wet brush.

Lines are thicker when drawn on wet paper (top).

Acrylic gouache.

# How to start drawing

Build up your Egyptian pictures in easy stages, starting with simple shapes and finishing with coloured crayons or paints. Try drawing the fish on this page, and the cat and the birds on pages 12–13, to get you started.

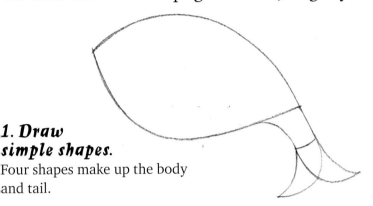

### 1. Draw simple shapes.
Four shapes make up the body and tail.

### 2. Work on the outline.
Look closely at the finished outline and work on it to give it a better shape and to make it look more real.

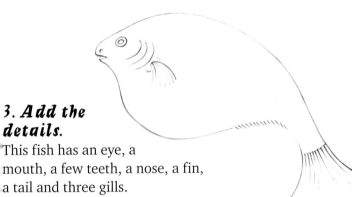

### 3. Add the details.
This fish has an eye, a mouth, a few teeth, a nose, a fin, a tail and three gills.

### 4. Put in the colour.
You could use crayons to build up the colour on the belly and on the back of the fish.

### 5. Add texture.
Small curved lines in black crayon give this fish a scaly texture on its back, and large and small brown dots give a mottled fishy skin texture on its belly. (A black crayon strengthens the lines already drawn on the fin, tail, eye, nose and teeth.)

### 6. Finish the drawing with a strong outline.
I've used a black crayon for this fish, but you can also use brown or dark red or a mix of these colours.

The fish and the cat come from paintings in the tomb-chapel of Nebamun, which are very lively and lifelike. You can see the full painting on pages 14–15.

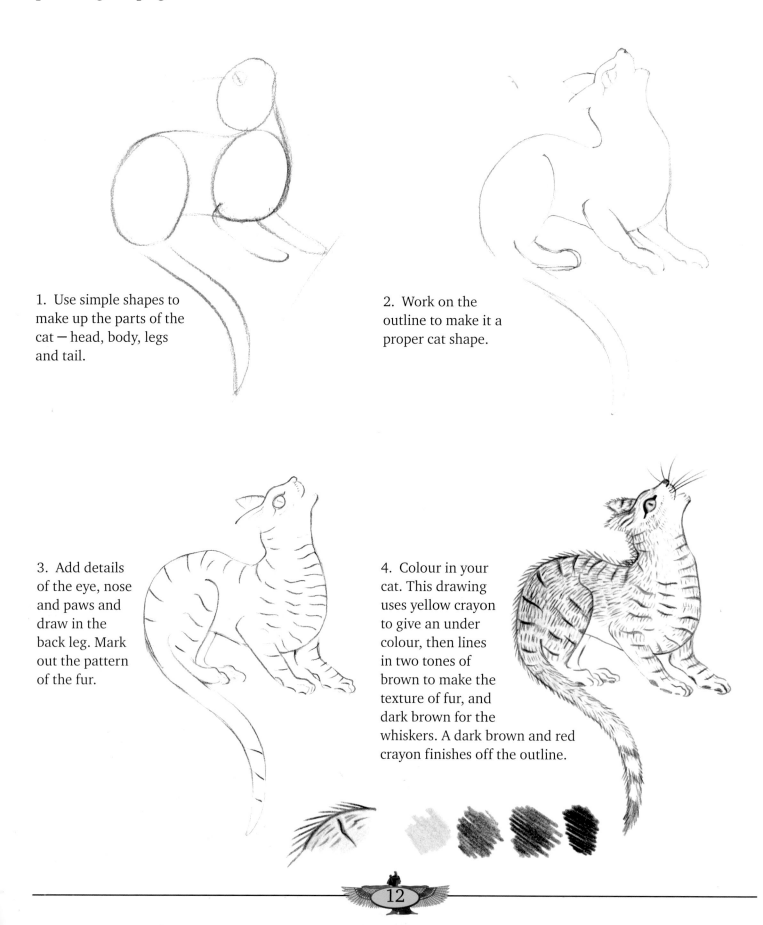

1. Use simple shapes to make up the parts of the cat — head, body, legs and tail.

2. Work on the outline to make it a proper cat shape.

3. Add details of the eye, nose and paws and draw in the back leg. Mark out the pattern of the fur.

4. Colour in your cat. This drawing uses yellow crayon to give an under colour, then lines in two tones of brown to make the texture of fur, and dark brown for the whiskers. A dark brown and red crayon finishes off the outline.

These birds are drawn in the same way as the cat, beginning with simple shapes for the head, body and wings, and building up to the finished drawing with a good outline, details and colour.

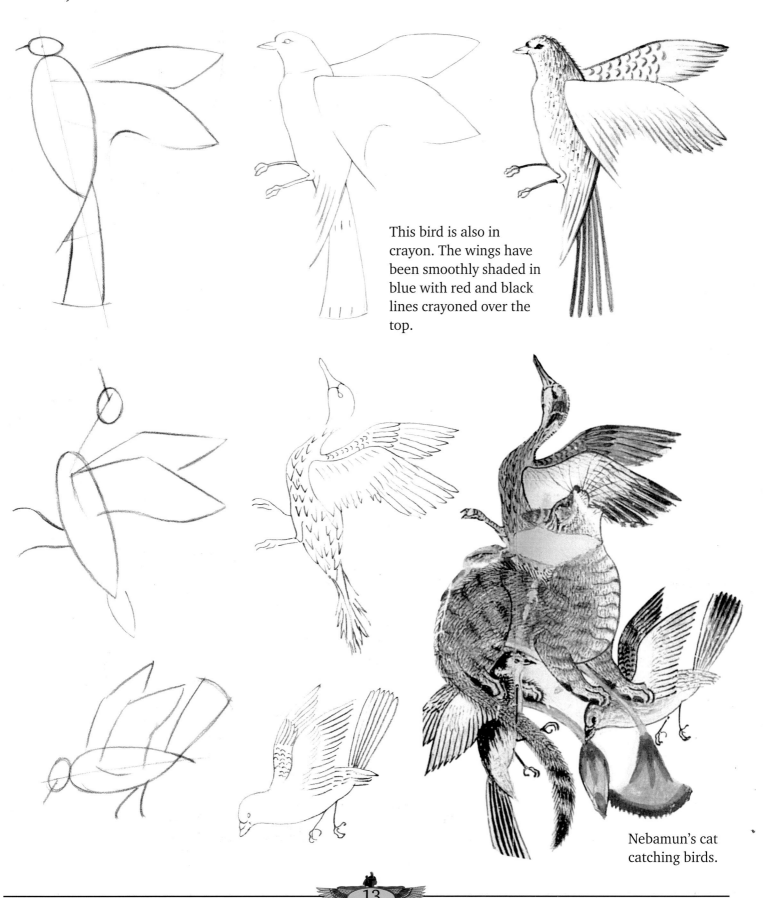

This bird is also in crayon. The wings have been smoothly shaded in blue with red and black lines crayoned over the top.

Nebamun's cat catching birds.

# Fowling in the marshes

This scene comes from the tomb-chapel of an official called Nebamun. You can see the fish, cat and birds from the previous three pages. Not all of the painting has survived. At the bottom left edge of the coloured painting you can just see part of a spear heading for the fish.

This clue, along with old photographs of two lost pieces of the painting, has allowed experts at the British Museum to make this reconstruction of the whole scene. The photographs show the top half of Nebamun holding more of the spear and Nebamun's daughter kneeling and holding a lotus flower. These are the grey shaded areas.

# Sacred animals

Crocodiles lived in the river Nile and were very dangerous to fishermen and people working and living near the river. The Ancient Egyptians feared crocodiles, but they also believed in the idea of getting the animals' ferocious power on their side for their own struggle against evil and danger. Crocodiles were the sacred animal of the god Sobek.

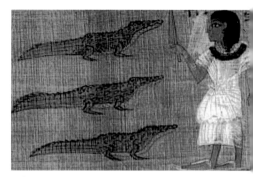

This ancient painting on papyrus shows Nakht controlling the power of the crocodiles.

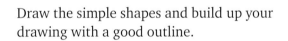

Draw the simple shapes and build up your drawing with a good outline.

This croc was painted in coloured inks mixed with water, then drawn over with an art pen to make the patterns on its scaly skin stand out and to add in the details. The outline of the croc and the pattern on the water were also drawn with an art-pen.

Inks are slightly transparent, so you can easily go over the pencil lines of your detailed drawing.

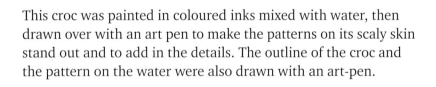

Hippos were often shown being hunted in the marshes. They were very dangerous to Egyptian farmers and destroyed their crops. The goddess Taweret was shown as a hippo. She was the goddess of pregnant women and childbirth.

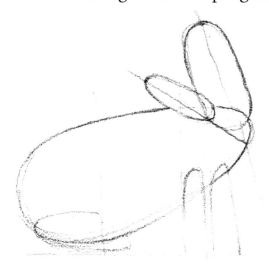

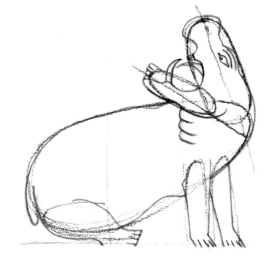

Draw the simple shapes, then add an outline and some details. You don't have to be too exact. After all, individual animals are a little different from each other – some are longer and some are fatter.

Colour and finish your drawing with a strong outline and details such as toes, eyes, eyebrows, ears, nostrils, tusks and teeth.

Hippos being hunted in the marshes.

The goddess Wadjit was shown as a cobra, often wearing the red crown of Lower Egypt. The goddess Nekhbet was shown as a vulture wearing the white crown of Upper Egypt. These two goddesses unite the two parts of Egypt, north and south.

Wadjit and Nekhbet on the coffin of Amun Amenemope.

Draw simple shapes for the head and body.

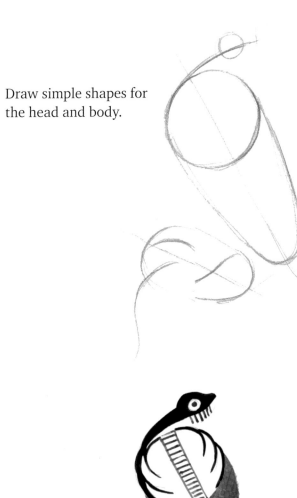

Then add more detail.

This cobra has been painted in watercolour.

The white lines for the feathers have been drawn in wax crayons with watercolours washed over the top.

Just four colours have been used for the cobra and the vulture.

Baboons were the sacred animals of Thoth, god of truth and wisdom. Here they are having fun in a tree and enjoying their favourite fruit.

Sketch simple shapes for the head, body and legs.

Draw in more details, adding eye, eyebrow, ear and mouth.

Make the baboon look real by adding colour and texture. Use long black lines to give the idea of long hair on its back and shorter lines for the hair over the rest of its body.

These baboons have been painted with inks and details added with a mapping pen.

A painting copied from a tomb at Beni Hasan.

## Baboons in a tree

1. Draw a circle and a square. Then draw the trunk inside the square and an even-looking arrangement of branches coming out of the trunk that roughly fits inside the circle.

2. Draw or trace the baboons. You may have to alter the branches so that the baboons look as if they are really sitting or standing on the branches.

3. Dot in figs and leaves all over your design and colour with paint or crayons.

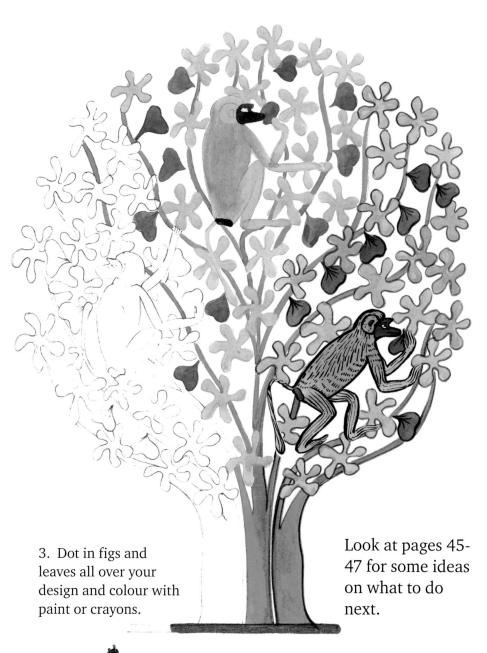

Look at pages 45-47 for some ideas on what to do next.

# People

Egyptian women and men were always drawn beautiful and young. Wives always sit or stand behind their husbands.

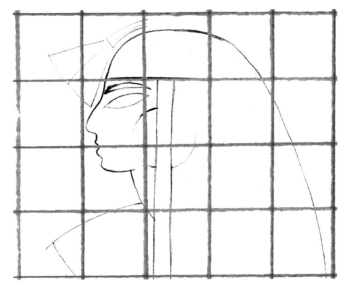

Grid = 5 x 4 squares.

Grids were used to make sure men, women and gods were drawn to the right scale. You can draw your own grid using a ruler and set-square, or use graph paper to copy this lady's head and shoulders. When you have copied her outline square by square, you might want to trace it onto watercolour paper, ready to paint. Notice that her head is wider than it is tall.

Work on getting a good outline and then put in more details. Her face is drawn from the side but the eyes and eyebrows are in front view. Her mouth has a pleased and calm expression. She wears her best jewellery and a fashionable cone of perfumed grease on top of her head.

This is painted in watercolour. The hair has been painted twice to make it a really deep black.

Red and black coloured pencils finish off the details and outline.

The same grid is used here so that you can compare the sizes and outlines of the head and shoulders of a woman, man and child. Men are drawn larger than women with their skin slightly redder and their necks thicker and shorter. Men's wigs are shorter and their shoulders are more square.

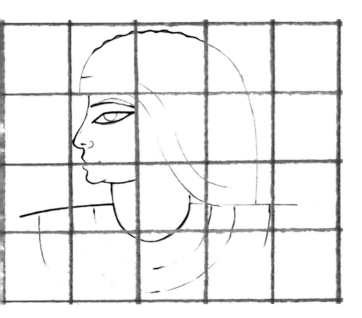

Children are much smaller, with pale skin like women. A hairstyle that shows part of their head indicates their youth.

Young woman with a bird, painted in a tomb at Deir el Medina.

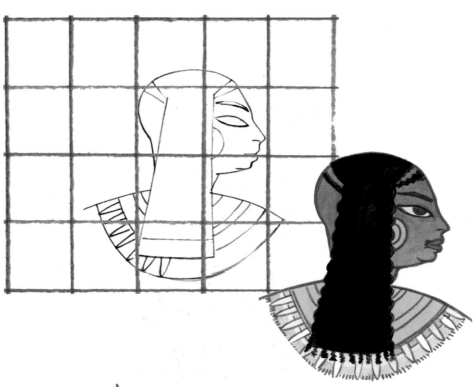

# Egyptians liked a party!

Here is a party scene from the tomb of Nebamun. The guests have plenty to eat and drink, and sweet-smelling cones on their heads. They hold lotus flowers.

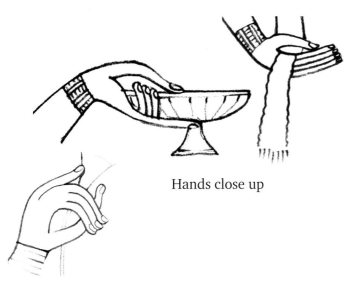

Hands close up

Colouring in

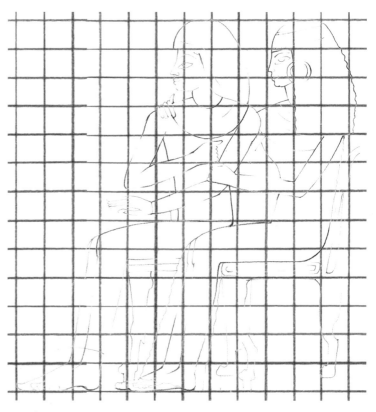

Grid = 13 x 13 squares.

This grid is here to guide you when drawing the seated couple.

The man's legs have been painted red. The woman's legs are paler. Under the cloth both have a lighter tone.
White lines have been drawn over their clothing and legs and a black outline added.

24

Rich Egyptians wore wigs, fine linen clothes and elaborate gold and coloured inlaid jewellery. Here are some examples.

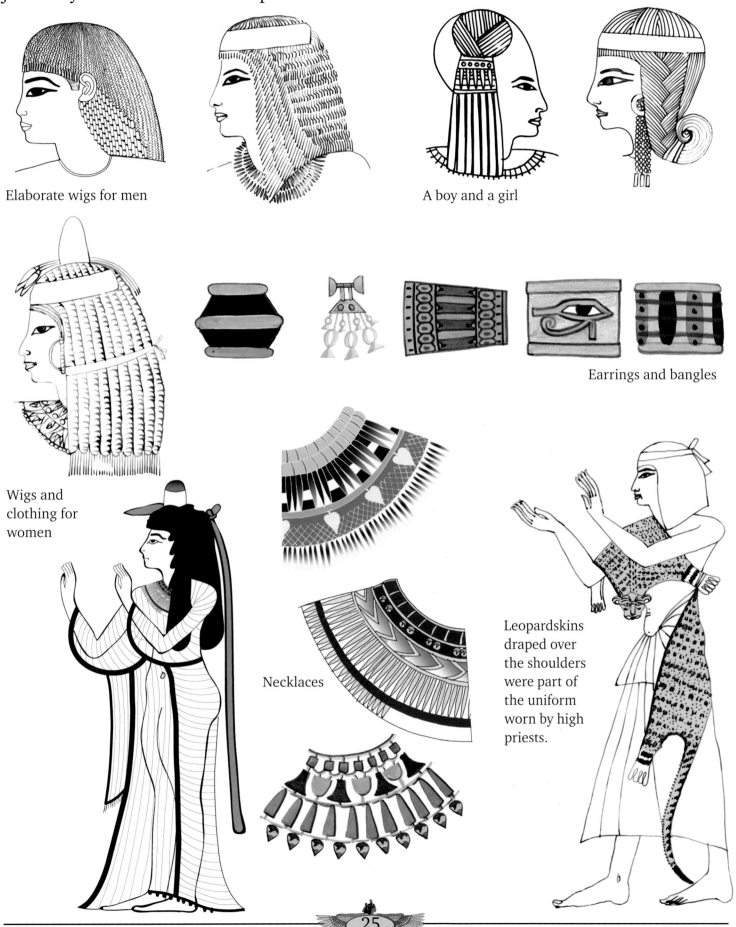

Elaborate wigs for men

A boy and a girl

Earrings and bangles

Wigs and clothing for women

Necklaces

Leopardskins draped over the shoulders were part of the uniform worn by high priests.

# Goddesses and gods

Goddesses looked similar to women, except that they were slightly taller and wore a divine symbol or crown on their heads. Their clothes were simple in shape and did not change with human fashions. A goddess's clothes stayed the same as when she was born at the beginning of the universe.

Isis and Nephthys stand behind the god of the dead, Osiris.

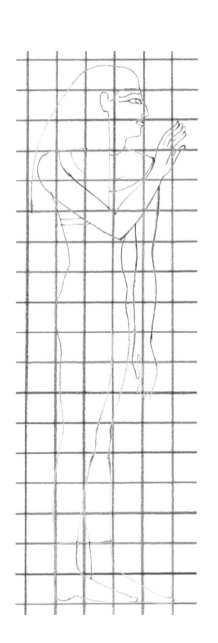

Isis, goddess of magic, wears her special symbol. It is usually painted green, the colour of rebirth.

Nephthys, goddess of the under-world, wears her special symbol.

Mut, the goddess of motherhood, wears a vulture headdress.

Hathor with King Seti. Hathor was the goddess of the west, where the sun set each day. Her symbol was a cow's horns carrying the sun. Hathor was the wife of Horus, the falcon-headed god.

Mix a flesh colour.

Select a range of colours to use for your goddess.

You may want to go over a watercolour wash again after it has dried to make a stronger colour.

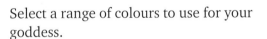

Close-up of Hathor and Seti's hands.

Hathor's symbol was the sun carried by cow's horns.

Hathor wears a dress covered in a beaded net. In each of the hexagonal shapes is a delicate hieroglyph.

The goddess Ma'at is shown below with outstretched wings that represent harmony and balance. The feather on her head represents truth and justice.

Grid = 22 x 8 squares.

You could draw your own grid and plot in her outline or use this grid to compare her height, and the length and size of her arms, legs and wings.

The Ancient Egyptians used a small range of colours for their paintings that gave a harmonious look. Try this for yourself. Mix your colours and work out a selection that you feel looks good together.

Gods were drawn the same as men but with the heads of animals that represented an idea or activity. For example, jackals lived in deserts and cemeteries so Anubis, with a jackal's head, is the god of embalming and magic.

The coffin of Pasenhor, showing the gods Thoth, Horus and Anubis. Anubis is weighing Pasenhor's heart. Horus is honouring Osiris, the god of the underworld, and Thoth is leading Pasenhor to the next life.

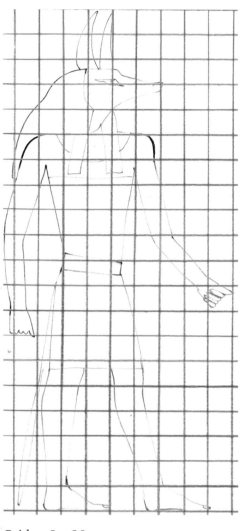

Grid = 9 x 20 squares.

Anubis

Thoth, the ibis headed god of wisdom and truth.

Khnum, the ram-headed god of potters.

Horus, the falcon headed god of day and night.

Seth, the god of conflict and chaos, has the head of a strange composite animal.

# Food for the offering table

Most Egyptian tomb walls show an abundant display of food laid out, either for the tomb owner to offer the gods, or as a feast to be enjoyed in the next life with friends and family.

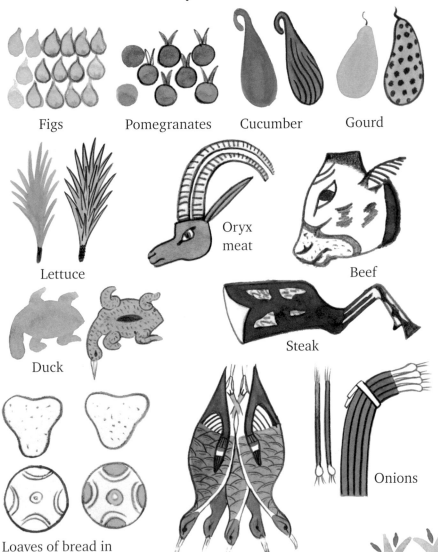

Figs

Pomegranates

Cucumber

Gourd

Lettuce

Oryx meat

Beef

Duck

Steak

Onions

Loaves of bread in different shapes.

Geese

Stela of Deniuenkhons, mistress of the house. She is offering beer, lettuce, bread, duck, figs and lotus flowers to the god Ra Horakhty.

A workman from Amarna enjoying a meal of bread, cucumbers and sweet onions.

## Create your own offering table

What food and drink would you include? Lotus flowers are especially important to cancel the strong smell of onions. For ideas, look at Nebamun's offering table on page 6 and the food inside the house on the opposite page.

Figs, grapes and lotus flowers.

# Homes and gardens

Houses were made from mud bricks covered with plaster and painted white. They had pretty pillars and roofed balconies. Colourful mats over windows and doors kept out sun and dust.

Drawings of Egyptian houses show front and inside views next to each other, but the proportions are not realistic. If a king or an important person is in a room, then that room is drawn very large. The servants are drawn very small. In the drawing below, we can see what the house looked like from the front, some of the activity inside, and the garden.

This is roughly what a real country house looked like.

The garden has fruit trees, grape vines and a sycamore tree.

Inside the house, guests have arrived. The hosts are ready with food and flowers.

The front shows three floors.

A well-dressed servant looks tired and thirsty after caring for the children.

One of the servants peeps unseen through a hole cut in the hanging mat.

Another servant brings a jar covered with an embroidered cloth.

# Design your own Ancient Egyptian house

This is another example of a busy house where servants make bread, clean and wash, sweep floors, play the harp, dance, sort out the business of the day and have a bite to eat.

## What would be happening inside your house?

Preparing for a party

Musicians

Flautists

The after-effects of a party!

Crafts-people, spinning and weaving

## What would your house look like from the outside?

A king's house with flags flying from the pillars.

Country houses

What would you put in your garden? Here are some ideas from temple and tomb walls.

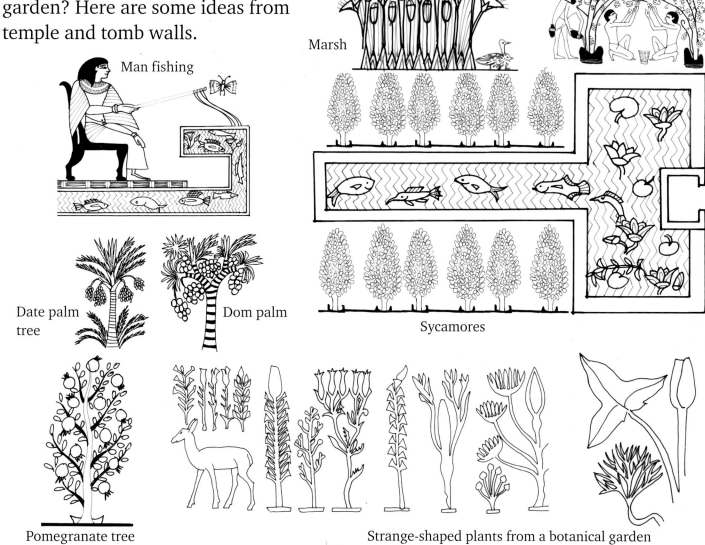

Man fishing

Marsh

Vines

Date palm tree

Dom palm

Sycamores

Pomegranate tree

Strange-shaped plants from a botanical garden

This house and garden have been painted with acrylic gouache on a sheet of papyrus.

# Working people

Important people were mostly drawn in formal poses, but working people were shown crouching, kneeling and bending to do all sorts of activities, from dancing to working in the fields. These two pages will help you practise drawing people using simple flat shapes. Figures working or at play look real enough, even though they are just flat shapes, because they have well-drawn details and are boldly drawn.

Over simple shapes draw outlines with curves around shoulders, elbows, wrists, chest, hips and legs. Look especially carefully at the knees, hands and feet.

This man is bending down to make mud bricks.

This man is pulling and twisting ends of a mesh bag to strain wine.

These men kneel and squat as they bring geese for their master Nebamun.

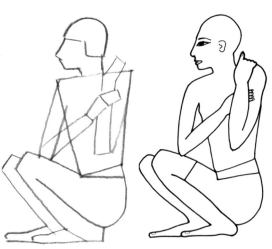

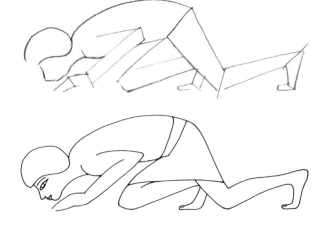

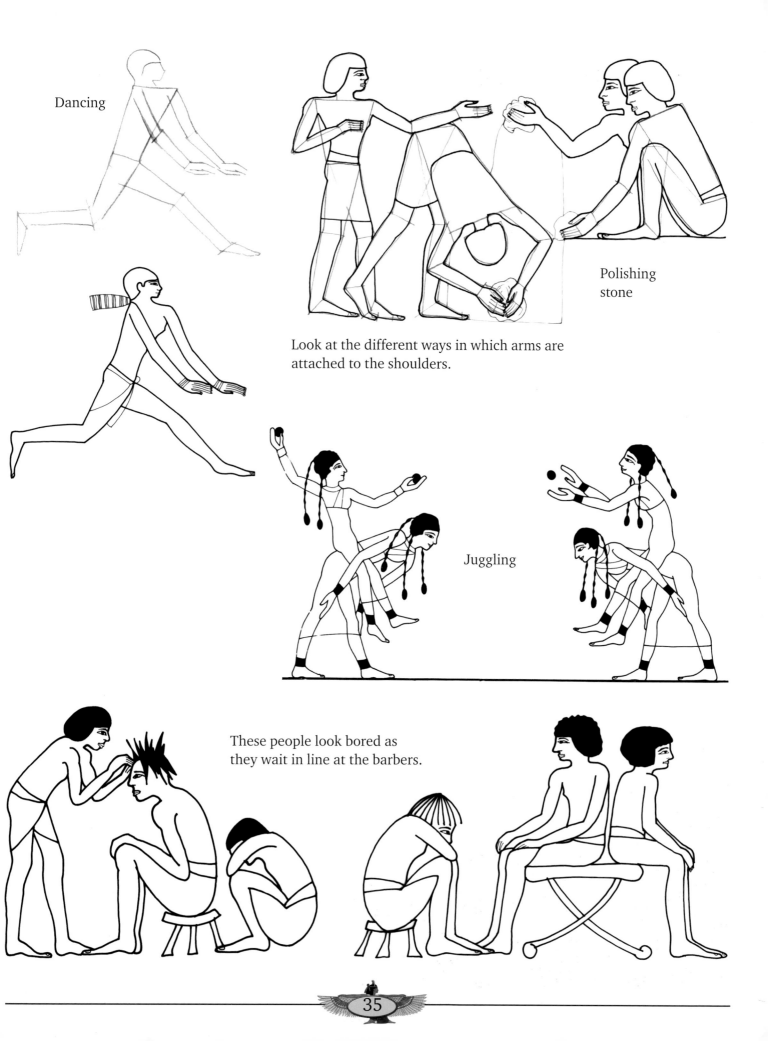

Dancing

Polishing stone

Look at the different ways in which arms are attached to the shoulders.

Juggling

These people look bored as they wait in line at the barbers.

# Composition

'False doors' were put in Egyptian tombs to link the dead to the living and as a place to make offerings. This false door was made for the priest Werirenptah. It has a formal arrangement. Register lines keep the sense of order and the pictures show some of the things needed for the afterlife. Plenty of people are bringing food for Werirenptah.

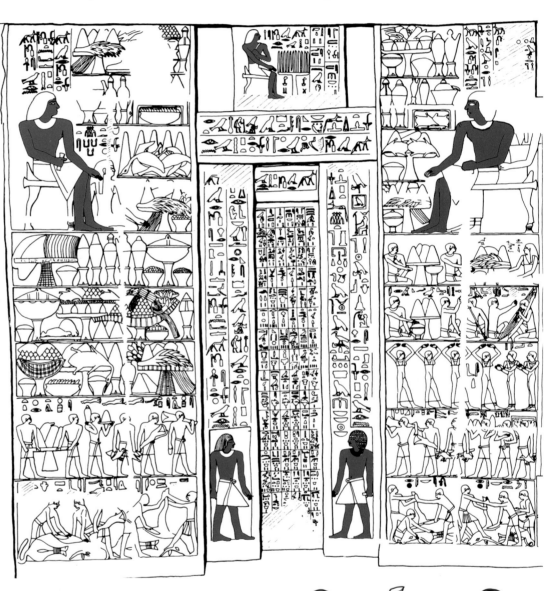

Werirenptah is shown five times.

On the left Werirenptah faces the false door with his wife at his feet. They have a pile of food on the table in front of them. Below are more vegetables and fruit, figs, grain and oils for the afterlife.

Werirenptah's men bring heavy loads of fowl and hunks of beef. At the bottom they are butchering animals so that Werirenptah will be able to feed all of his family and staff.

On the right, Werirenptah's wife sits beside him and both face towards the false door with more offerings before and below them. They want to party in the next life so they have musicians, dancers and clapping accompanists.

Men butchering a cow.

The false door on this page comes from the chapel wall inside Nakht's tomb (Nakht also appears on page 5). This is a less formal composition showing farming activities. Men harvest, measure and separate the wheat from the chaff with Nakht (seated) looking on.

The large standing figures of Nakht and his wife face the other way, towards the offering table where Nakht adds to an already full table by pouring more grain. There is a butcher at work and a man holding purifying incense.

At the bottom Nakht watches ploughing in an unusual and free-flowing farming scene with a winding riverbed that has dried up apart form a small pond. It also shows sowing, ploughing and cutting down trees. In the bottom left corner, a thirsty man is taking a drink from a goat-skin water bottle hung in the cool of a tree.

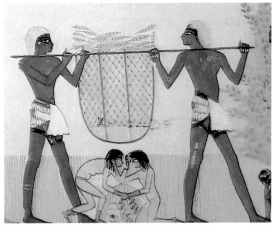

Workers were not always shown being well behaved. The artists liked to add a little bit of realism. Here, two girls are pulling each other's hair!

# Foreign and exotic animals

Here is a painting of men from Nubia and Syria bringing all kinds of exotic animals to the temple of Ramesses II. They bring bulls, an oryx, a lion, gazelles, a cheetah, a monkey, an ostrich, and hunting dogs as well as elephant tusks, animal skins and ostrich eggs.

In the famous temple of queen Hatshepsut there are pictures of some of the animals that were brought to the queen from the land of Punt, in Africa. Other unusual and exotic animals can be found in other Ancient Egyptian carvings and paintings.

This monkey has been drawn using water-soluble crayons dipped in water and worked quickly over a pencil sketch.

The giraffe has been painted in yellow watercolour. The dark red markings were added with crayons.

A young boy looking after a bird, monkey and baboon.

An elephant and a bear being led by a Syrian man.

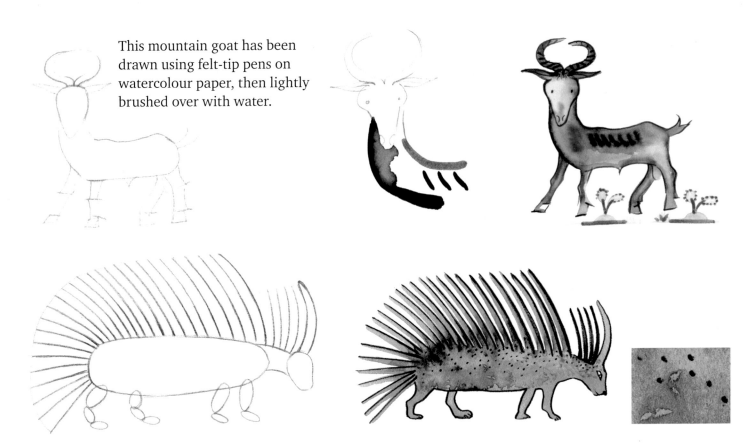

This mountain goat has been drawn using felt-tip pens on watercolour paper, then lightly brushed over with water.

This porcupine has been drawn with crayon and watercolour on wet paper.

A sharpened 4B pencil has been used to draw this cheetah.

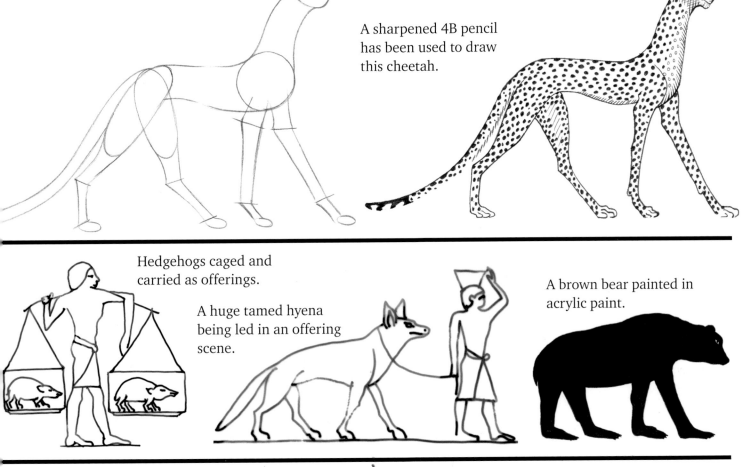

Hedgehogs caged and carried as offerings.

A huge tamed hyena being led in an offering scene.

A brown bear painted in acrylic paint.

Many creatures in Egyptian mythology were mixtures (or 'composites') of two or more beasts or beings, which combined different qualities such as fierceness and wisdom. The Egyptians thought such creatures lived in the desert or in the underworld. Here are some examples.

This is the 'devourer', called Ammut, made up of crocodile, lion and hippo. She is always ready to gobble up an evil heart. Before entering the underworld, everyone had to be judged and his or her heart weighed against a feather of Thoth.
(See page 28 for a picture of a judgement scene.)

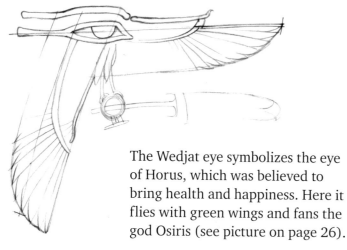

The Wedjat eye symbolizes the eye of Horus, which was believed to bring health and happiness. Here it flies with green wings and fans the god Osiris (see picture on page 26).

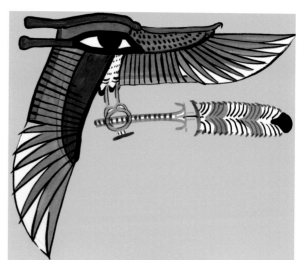

This is the kind tree goddess, who offers food and drink to help the dead in the underworld.

The *ba* is the spirit of the deceased, which has a person's head and features combined with the body and wings of a falcon. A *ba* can pass swiftly between the worlds of the living and the dead.

This coffin shows the goddess Hathor as a cow stepping out of the hills of Thebes to welcome the deceased's *ba*.

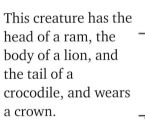

This creature has the head of a ram, the body of a lion, and the tail of a crocodile, and wears a crown.

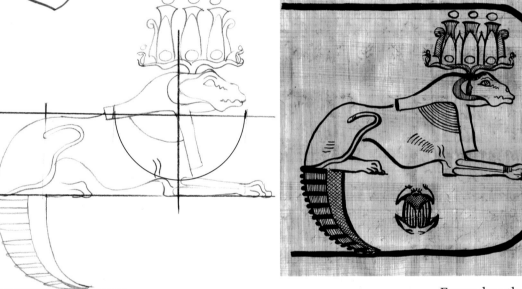

Every day, the scarab beetle must push the sun up from the underworld, so that a new day can dawn.

Various mythical tales and pictures were written on papyri and placed in the tombs of the dead.

Snakes and serpents had a great part to play in Ancient Egyptian myths. This one has attributes of a human, a lion, a jackal and a bird. It carries the sun between its wings.

On these sheets of papyri I have used black and red gouache paint and an art pen for the fine lines.

# A comical papyrus

Look at these sketches of animals doing human activities.

These are fun to copy and sketch and you don't have to be too exact. Draw with quick and bold movements to match the look of the cartoon characters.

Water-soluble graphite pencils have been used on this page. They come in different tones (8B is very dark and 2B is much lighter). Dipping the tip of the pencils in water makes a strong dark line and watercolour can be brushed over the line when dry.

# Ideas for what to do next

Get into the habit of carrying a sketchbook with you when out and about and visiting a museum. Make quick sketches of things that catch your eye or imagination. Copying things really makes you look at them, and you nearly always see something new that you hadn't noticed at first. You can add colour or make your own designs or mixed-up creatures later when you have more time.

Be inspired by something you saw at a museum (like this hippo carved on a shrine) and do your own thing.

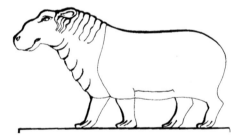

Make a quick sketch and add colour later. This animal design is found on Tutankhamun's dagger case.

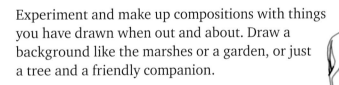

Experiment and make up compositions with things you have drawn when out and about. Draw a background like the marshes or a garden, or just a tree and a friendly companion.

Try creating the look of papyrus by using water-soluble crayons. Crayon in lines both up and down the paper then use a soft broad brush to wash over the area with water so that you have an even colour. Leave some of the crayon marks to show through. Wait until it is dry, then draw and paint on top.

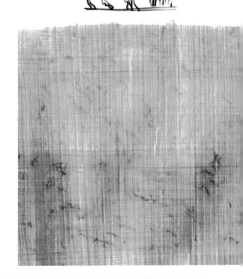

# Make cards for family and friends or invitations to a party or 'get together'.

HUMOROUS Birthday card
(see page 20).

GLAMOROUS Invitation for a 'girls'
night in' (see hands and faces on
page 25).

MYSTERIOUS postcard to send to a
mate (see page 43).

## *Try a different technique*

Cut and paste paper onto card and add lines using tubes of sticky glitter glue paint. Squeeze the tubes as evenly as you can along the edges of the paper and on the details for the bread, duck, figs etc. Use the offering table on page 30 to give you ideas.

Ancient Egyptian paintings appear quite flat and so they are very good to make into designs of shapes, patterns and colours.

Try wax crayons with ink over the top. They are quick and fun to use together.

Potato prints

Use your designs to decorate all kinds of things - boxes, pottery, a border or frieze for a room. Make a lino cut or print some cloth using fabric paint and potatoes.

Whatever you do, the important thing is to experiment, practise your skills at drawing and painting and enjoy being creative.

Cut your own stencils.

# Further Reading

Serval cat

*Ancient Egyptian Designs* by Eva Wilson, British Museum Press 1986

*Arts and Crafts of the Ancient World: Ancient Egypt* by Ting Morris, Dorling Kindersley 2006

*Eyewitness Guides: Ancient Egypt* by George Hart, Dorling Kindersley 1990

*Illustrated Atlas of Ancient Egypt* by Delia Pemberton, British Museum Press 2005

*Illustrated Encyclopaedia of Ancient Egypt* by Geraldine Harris and Delia Pemberton, British Museum Press (2nd edition 2005)

*Kingdom of the Dead - Voyages through Time* by Peter Ackroyd, Dorling Kindersley 2004

*Pocket Dictionary of Ancient Egyptian Gods and Goddesses* by George Hart, British Museum Press 2001

*Pocket Dictionary of Ancient Egyptian Animals* by Angela McDonald, British Museum Press 2004

*Story of the Nile* by Dr Anne Willard, illustrated by Steve Noon, Dorling Kindersley 2003

*The Tomb of Nebamun* by Meredith Hooper, British Museum Press (forthcoming 2008)

A fox raiding a bird's nest

Hedgehogs eating a locust

An ichneumon hungry for ducklings